WHEN ALL ELSE FAILS WALK ON WATER

WHEN ALL ELSE FAILS WALK ON WATER

Growing In Faith

DERRICK LACY

Derrick Lacy
When All Else Fails Walk On Water

Published by Spines

ISBN: 979-8-89569-425-1

When All Else Fails:

The very language of Heaven when we ask of God is No, or Yes, or Not right now. Our conversation with Him concerning what we ask for should be specific. This is approached with confidence. Of course, our minds are prone to wander and target doubt! "If" should never be in our vocabulary because "if" breeds doubt. It pleases our Father to bless us at our request. He rewards us when we carefully seek Him. But "Faith" must be the ingredient to receive Him. All this information so far is based on scriptures derived from the Bible.

- Matt. 5:37; 7:7-11
- Phil. 4:6
- Heb. 4:15
- Rom. 4:20-22

- Matt. 21:21, 22
- Heb. 11

Joseph is a perfect example of a God-fearing man who was optimistic about his misfortunes. The fact that there was a good chance for him to get out of prison the first possible time through a good recognition, and it hadn't should've been a time to give up on God or any opportunity of getting out. But he continued in the things of God. He was kept in Perfect Peace. He didn't grow weary at all during as the scriptures bid us to not do.

- Gen. 39:3, 4; 20-23; 40:12-15; 23, 41:9-13; 25-33, 37-42; 45:4-8

Jesus followed after the nature of Joseph and was optimistic as well, showing forgiveness. This was looking to the brighter side of things, knowing that God had an underlying purpose in the situation where it seemed He was not available.

Stephen had the same attitude of forgiving his oppressors, Acts 7:59, 60. We must believe that in all things, whether favorable or bad, God can and will make a way out of what seems to be against our better judgment.

Rom. 8:1. David said,

> "Never once have I seen the righteous forsaken,"
>
> Prov. 14:9; Ps. 37:25, 26.

Failure could arise from a broken moment based on our effort, but God's opportunity to do His part to birth a miracle. It becomes a moment where man's extremities become God's opportunity. When we release our faith, God hurries it to where He moves toward bringing our desires to reality. This is us doing our part; then the Lord does His part to send it. His stamp of approval is on our request because the faith we exercised compelled God to move towards us. When it may seem that it's something that we're doing (that's wrong) or something that we're not doing, nor need God's approval, be encouraged to know that God looks past our faults and sees the need to heal us by answering our request. Ps. 19:1-14; 69:13-22; Ps. 133:3; 8-12. Men may lock one door, but God sends you to open others. Men may try to stop God's will for our lives but come up short. Man attempts may slow the process but cannot stop it. It won't or can't stop the movement of God. His plans work without fault, and we're highly favored by Him. 1 Cor. 2:9; Isa. 55:8-11.

When All Else Fails

"Success" can be determined on a small scale as being able to get up out of bed to do our hygiene. Simple chores around the house or place of stay and those little acts of duties can have wins in the past give us comfort. Having confidence gives us the drive to start out moving forward. "Confidence" is a strong booster which is a product of one who plans and sets goals. And for the most part, if we don't set goals, we can be tempted to remain or stay at a certain level of achievement, yielding the opportunity to raise the bar, so to speak. This can allow us to grow to a form, which can rob us of precious time and room to grow. Many great leaders in the Bible were called out from family and friends to seek a higher calling found in Him. There's also cases in the scriptures where family is included.

Note: "Thackley." Knowing when to move or stay is solely based on our relationship with our Father God. Beside this area checked off, we can look and expect God to guide us step by step. When we know that we're in God's will (even on a small scale), no form of illusion can lead us differently. The forces of darkness will seek people, places, and things to discourage us because they know that we're on the right path. And we can influence others to come. Gen. 12:1-3; 13:1, 2, 6:13.

It's a natural thing to be frustrated when our plans don't become a reality. It's confusing to try and figure out how the Lord operates the same with anything for that matter. Many leaders get upset with God because they aren't convinced of how He will, in His own time, bring deliverance to a thing. Jonah was one who, after his three days of suffering, was unwilling to do God's will and run to the battle, so to speak. Then got mad because he could see another way to bring about His order. Jonah 1:1. The prophet Elijah complained after enduring a mighty work for the Lord and lost focus for a moment. This tempted him to focus on only his self-worth or what he brought to the table. Comparing himself with people, places, and things which can bring about a lack of understanding. Like many, God knows like an iron that begins to melt, He desires to tell them to do His good bidding because following keeps us protected like His outstretched hands. He doesn't allow one thing to go without value. The question we ask is why don't we ask more than "Will you keep in mind everything about Him?"

> Ps. 8:4-9. His timing is perfect. I will still hold faith in the things He said for us,

> Ps. 89:1, 9-12. Many are our afflictions but God will deliver us from them all as the scripture says.

> Ps. 34:19, 22. Let us continue to trust in the Lord by learning our waiting to pass. Let us not grow weary in our efforts.

> Then we apply the goodness of God. Ps. 37:5, 2 Thes. 3:13.

If we are confused, rest assured the sources from our efforts which fall under the heading of spiritual wickedness. God doesn't promote distractions, especially when His plan is to provide for us. Our thoughts are pronounced by humanly exaggerated fears of not knowing. We can create within ourselves the forces of darkness which makes their job easier. The enemies of forces of darkness try to influence us to give up trusting in the things of God to hold us captive against our will. It's one thing to be locked up physically, but far more vital to be confined in our thinking because circumstances and situations attack us. This can make it hard for us to see the hand of God in our lives. The main objective is to force us to believe that God is our problem. The forces of darkness have three main areas to target in our lives to try and create a pattern of thinking and discredit God:

1. In the area of our finances. Not having enough money to cover all our expenses alone can bring us to a tailspin. It can lead us to try get rich schemes that can help dig a bigger hole for us. Not being able to provide for our families can rob us of our respect and stability.

2. Our health can be next. A turn for the worse to cause us to curse God. These things can wrestle us to the ground to have us questioning our own purpose in life.

"Why Me Lord?" can easily roll off of our lips to yield us saying things we would rather take back.

3. Last on the hit list is: The harm that can come to our family and friends (leading to hospitalization or death). This can force us to care unguided, especially if we're worried not to be there for them. We then pull out

our last drop and permit ourselves to kick ourselves in the head repeatedly. This becomes a very, very unhealthy predicament. This opens the door for the blame game to stick its ugly head out, which is a demonic spiral first introduced in the Garden of Eden. Gen. 3:9, 15, 2 Cor. 11:4, 1 Pet. 5:7-11, Phil. 1:14.

The father of the sick child told Jesus,

> "I believe but help me with the rest of my belief."
>
> Mark 9:23-24, KJV.

This was the right move or attitude taken by the father who recognized the area of doubt in his life. We are allowed to walk the walk of faith in our weaknesses and in faith so that the rest of the help we need, being prayerful and in denial, can push us to our wins. We have to let those wins overcome the failures.

The spirit of worrying can and will rob us of peace with God through Jesus. It can bring unwanted weight to us as believers. Heb. 12:1-3. Life is a one-time race here before life and death.

So, begin to want it, own it. Our life and example will

lead others to Christ. Don't let the excuses, "I didn't make it good," to Prov. 11:30-31.

"Life" is what we make it. It's a race where to be a winner requires us to finish it. God gives us a start by being born. And in this early stage of life, we have our tutors and trainers whom God has given us called parents. Family and friends help shape our character, too. It doesn't matter what place we come in—we should just focus on finishing the race. We only have one life here on this earth, but we learn responsibility, more or less. We are to develop our spiritual nature for positive results as we work in stages. Life's lessons can and will teach us. Giving us awareness. We then can choose to repeat the cycle of an unhealthy outcome or choose to allow it to be a learning experience. Habits that are bad can cause life's experiences we call vicious cycles. But don't be afraid to make mistakes. We all are born in the school of hard knocks, not by choice. Some bumps and bruises are needful and some are unnecessary. But it's essential that we grow.

When All Else Fails

How much emphasis is placed on life?

How do we measure the value of a life?

Do we measure "Life" by quantity or quality?

Is "Life" considered a good one viewed by length of years, whether one had bad health or what? One thing we can rest assured, it's highly precious in the eyes of our Creator. He made us in His likeness and image. There was a ransom to be paid for every human being, and Jesus paid it all. We were walking the Green Mile, so to speak, until Jesus got us off Death Row.

The Word says that:

> "Life is like a vapor or fine mist of steam that quickly evaporates. The only time it is picked up, it's no longer 'Here Today, Gone Tomorrow,' it is now 'Here Today, Gone Today!'"

The question was asked by Jesus, "What will one give in exchange for their soul?" The spectrum comes from money, drugs, or selfish sale. But the truth of the matter is, our souls are God's. Business and life only lead us to choose where our souls spend eternity. The mind is our eye gate to the entrance to our soul and our mind. Decisions will determine where our souls spend eternity. We bring up children in the knowledge of God. We become and should become responsible parents, building family values, as they were passed on to us, whether poorly or not.

Mark 8:36-38, 1 Tim. 3:1-2, Jas. 4:13-15, Lk. 18:15-24, Col. 1:15-22.

And by our example, our children follow our lead. We live by a common rule which is warped and passed on. It goes like: "Do as I say and not as I do." The parent takes little stock in the nature that the children are prone to follow with a strong influence of what they see their parents do more than what they hear them say. This is because actions speak louder than words! So, a highly concerned prayer would be for the parents' actions to line up with their ground rules. Jesus bid the disciples to not stop the kids from coming, but let them come. He will teach them. He said for such are His kingdom—meaning very precious in His sight. And I bid them to them, even inside the penalty of death. Also, with the elderly. We're far about once a child, twice needing to be led at some point in time. So, to absorb all this information should encourage us that God has our best interest at heart. Make no mistakes about it! His covering and love is provided at our disposal. We can have our own securities keeping us from hurts and dangers, but because of the fall of man in the garden, death has become the last enemy to be defeated.

Why does God allow the forces of darkness to hang around? The accusations started in heaven before the world. Now they are on earth.

1 Cor. 15:52-57, Isa. 14:12-15, Ezek. 28:3-19, Matt. 18.

When All Else Fails

God the Father created everything to perfection, which is His very nature. Isa. 1:17. He created the angels for fellowship to give Him company. There was harmony and unity in Heaven. God wasn't and isn't selfish in His act of making us for praise. He revealed to us His character by including us in His worship, showing us how to appreciate authority that has our best interest at heart. All this began in Heaven before He even created the world and mankind. Gen. 1:25, 26. Fellowship or unity was important among the angelic hosts in Heaven as well in every being that's looking forward to being successful. Agreement is vital to prove that one is on the same page. That lets us know that we are a team. But fellowship was broken when God was accused of "slavery!" It was said of Him making us as robots to do praise, out of us against our will. The Creator was accused of not giving the angels a choice to worship God or not. The debate or argument was that they were relegated to excessive "free-will," so out of a loving God. The Creator allowed the angels to exercise their free-will. This led 1/3 of the angels to form an allegiance with Lucifer, who only wanted to be praised and in charge. God began exercising His love in this manner by not sheltering us fully from being tempted to do evil or wrong. What in the beginning He made fit to where the angels did not know what it was to rebel or cause division.

Isa. 14:12-15, Jer. 14:7, 2 Pet. 3:9, Mal. 3:6, Ezek. 28:1, 17.

He gave us free-will which gave us the opportunity to show our love for God. To appreciate Him by obeying Him. We love God by obeying Him. This works into the world of parenting as well. Our parents gave us rules and chores to do around the house that they expect us to enforce. For the most part, their purpose is to help us grow up in life to be responsible. Giving us a foundation to be respected in society and become a product of what our parents hope to show: good, positive family values. The ground rules that a parent may expect of us may seem hard or overbearing, but we know that it was to prepare us to be responsible. We may find it hard and burdensome in the early stages of bringing joy to our parents by doing what pleases them. But if we grow to do what pleases them out of free will, we begin to love them even more. Their reflection in our lives, where our family values and convictions keep us from falling into bad habits. We learn to appreciate the way we've been raised just like with our earthly parents. It pleases God to see us reflect His character over evil. Exercising our free-will to serve Him. Even still, free-will at times is under attack. Being accused of forcing His will upon the angels (i.e., like humans) had like caused us later compelled Him to prove to us that His is love. When He (being God) didn't have to prove anything to us. But then, the very existence of our free-will either for good or bad will prove to all the universe that there is no space except through the means of free will.

Prov. 3:12, Job 5:17, Job 4:19, Jn. 17:23, 1 Cor. 4:9, Rev. 14:6-9.

When All Else Fails

In the beginning, the glory of God was shared with all Heaven with Him being the power source. This meaning, His glory being light was so radiant, it filled the whole Heavenly. And those that were in His presence were exposed to where His glory reflected off of them. As long as there was unity, the glory of God rested upon every being in Heaven. Lucifer and the other angels were created to join in the glory of God. The Father gave Lucifer renown by giving him a position as the lesser light of His glory. In short, Lucifer because of his beauty and wisdom, he got power drunk. He got to imagining that he could govern things better around Heaven by changing things up a bit. This was a means of getting beside himself.

Isa. 14:13, 14, Ezek. 28:12, 15, 17.

He even accused the Most High and acted in a sense of putting God on trial (or in check) as if The Father was indicted. He was on trial for "slavery," traffic and holding the very things of (Jude's angels). The scripture Ezek. 28:18. Who would imagine that God, the righteous Judge of all, would be accused and put on trial for questioning His character, which is His law? Ps. 50:6. Everything about God and His way about doing things (His commandment) was under check when Lucifer went about starting a rally to promote his rule.

His influence was so convincing, he strengthened his arm by signing one-third of the host in Heaven. This got him banned from lodging in Heaven, left to wander needing permission to enter its border like we enter other countries needing a passport. God allowed him and the angelic actions to cast themselves in outer darkness, which later became the world we live in today.

Gen. 1:2. His actions and strike in Heaven cast about before The Father made human life on earth. To later discover that the unique new God formed, a being resembling Him in looks and character, made it a more complicated attack, seeing that he was going to have to find a way to manipulate His creation (Adam and Eve) to gain dominion and authority on earth. Once again, Lucifer, who became Satan (meaning deceiver, adversary, enemy of God), was up to his tricks. He was jealous of God to a degree of wanting to change or overthrow His rule or system. And to witness The Father create an earth figure that represents His order of things added to his hatred. Satan's mindset was dead set to rebel against the higher authority (God) and he could be crowned the god of this world. Even though he was against The Father's way of doing things, Satan studied God's nature thoroughly to carefully [lead] the world astray by degrees of counterfeit. In order to pass off a lie or false concept, one must add in certain amounts of truth to it. Gen. 1:26-28.

When All Else Fails

Just like The Heavenly Father's glory filled heaven, so was its presence in the Garden of Eden. He gave Adam (man) dominion or authority to replenish the earth. To get Adam to rebel against God was the next plan of action. Fellowship is what kept harmony in the garden, and as long as Adam and Eve were in agreement with The Father, they could experience the presence of God up close and personal. Even the animals experienced the glory of God, which gave them harmony with Adam, who named them one by one.

Note: When there is a breakdown in the chain of command, it affects the whole—from the greatest to the least. Even the innocent world of animals suffers, being a victim of circumstances. When Adam and Eve gave in to the lie, they exposed themselves to failure. And the presence of God became an atmosphere that slowly left their presence. One poor decision led to another, the act of rebellion was bred through their eyes that caused the first murder to take place. The very first nature to do right by God now became a behavior that needed to be taught instead of being genetically passed on. "Rebellion" became an inherited trait which transcends against God's nature, character, law, commandments, etc. Gen. 4:8-15, 1 Sam. 15:22-23.

God created everything with a formula or way that kept things simple. His blueprint or design was perfect; no need in altering. The whole atmosphere from Heaven to earth showed that God's plan for man and creature was one that could reproduce after itself. And even after the Fall of Man, The Father made provisions (a way) for us to return or get back in fellowship with Him. This was through animal sacrifices. The blood of animals (just like the worst of its other) animals provided atonement. The scriptures tell us that without the shedding of blood (animal sacrifices), there's no forgiveness or price to be paid for the violation. Someone had to die (pure and innocent) in replace of the wrongful deed. And this was the ritual or way of life until Jesus opened it all with His one ultimate act on Calvary. The pure blood innocent for the violators. This act showed God's love towards us and

Jesus' love for volunteering to be put to death. This just led up to the individual (by choice) to accept the offering, which allowed us to move forward to God to once again allow us to be in harmony with our Creator. This was a very simple plan, but the consequences tempted man to continue in sin, hiding and being in denial because of our actions. This is what "sin" does. Man's complicated life can lead to the opposite effect: running from God instead of to Him.

When All Else Fails

God is the definition of "Love." "Love" is the ideal covering that decorated everything The Father made. The very language of Love gives us the free-will to commune with God. The love of God covers a multitude of sins, which also leads to repentance. And by knowing that God is the same yesterday, today, and forever as the scripture says, it lets me know that Lucifer had time to think about what he had in mind to do. God gives us space to repent. He always sends warnings before executing His judgment. This lets me know that Lucifer had made up his mind and the mark he wanted to be the one calling the shots, made it harder to resist the opportunity to try and overthrow God's judicial system. But the only way this would work was to discredit God and at the same time mimic The Father's actions. He recognized that

God had well-planned things for His glory, but his wisdom and beauty clouded his judgment. He coveted God, which means to be that being and to want what that being had—which was the ruler of the universe. Note: What a person can do with free-will once the mind is made up and can get the job done and promote organizations.

Ezek. 19:1-12, Job 4:18, 1 Pet. 4:8, Prov. 10:12, Rom. 2:4, Heb. 13:8, Mal. 3:6.

The art of counterfeit is one that follows or lacks amount of coverage appears to merit a professional observance. There's a possibility that common evaluation can be manipulated. Meaning, experts look for certain flaws that average people have either keyed to overlook. Anything that is used to show the viewer to believe that an object is genuine or real when it is not, is said to be false or fake. An object most closely resembles the original, and this becomes easier when one uses materials and pieces that stem from the original. Falsified statements mixed with true statements confuse the public that were intended to figure it out. The times that we live in now are the end times where right is being seen as wrong, and wrong as right. What's popular is considered unpopular in the eyes of those who are selfish or in denial about it. As Paul says it best, God chooses the foolish things of the world to confound or confuse the wise. Meaning, the average-thinking person (or one that seeks the approval of others) that considers taking time out for spiritual things (such as seeking God) isn't of grave importance, finding it hard to understand how simple things are the key to a successful term on earth by people who are considered uneducated.

1 Cor. 1:21, 1:25-29.

Walk on Water

MATT. 14:25-29

As I see the days numbering, my life is growing to be more of a walk on water. I don't trust the things around me that I see. The things I hear are just fabricated rumors. It's just a B-movie that never made it far to be a Grammy, with its players rusty with their acting. The sacrifice for this righteous noble cause will get someone stoned to death. This is as if one's character is being assassinated. This world is an upside-down kingdom, meaning evil is esteemed greatly versus good. Being noble is obsolete, and quickness has reached heaven! But what about me? I can make a difference as I continue to walk on water. There are those of us who are last of a dying breed. Yes, there's thieves in the temple serving as rulers. There's a certain amount of honor among thieves that seem to be at bay. There's a war going on and I didn't start it, but there are those of us who are on the front line. Who will finish it? We need more reformers in this closing of Earth's history, holding up prayer forces above to send God's harvesters to usher in the last day's battle. One more thing: the battle isn't ours, or we are defeated, but they were those who had read the last pages. We have to fight even if we don't want to. So, let's make it a good one. Our integrity is at stake.

We have a heavenly host of angels such as ourselves, which are few but many. Our weapons are more advanced than due credit. I've been picked out to be picked on, and I have made the decision to quit giving my power to business and to things of unholiness. My eyes are in my head to see that the rain is gone. I'm seeing it as a battle that is won by influence, by way of our character. There are so many "Doubting Thomases" that will witness the beauty of it all through people that have finally realized that it's what we do that's the changing tool. This is because people want to see things work for us before they exercise it in their diet of things. People who expect more out of us than they do of themselves. Onward Christian Soldier! As I continue to walk on water, I see things flying around influencing people on all levels. May we stop these things before it develops within us inside-out. May I call a spade a spade. Even though we're under a curse, let's reverse it. Life can be a smoother race even though some can't swim in this "race of life," we should learn to swim, then we can learn to walk on water.

Everything that shines has value, but it only lures or attracts. Life is more than meets the eye, and all things heard approach with caution. All this may save us from a decision on life, but the life we save may be our own. Let's take a recap to where it all began. In a garden named Eve, a couple of humans took matters into their own hands that caused a snowball effect up to our present day. Life began hard but fair because Heaven provided an alternative all we had to do was stop, drop, and submit. This gave us a plan of salvation, which was the key to the city. We now have a license to destroy works of dishonesty to bring justice to a dying world. We have lost many casualties but to gain because we have far to die is a gain. Let's give the people something to live for by dying (leaving a legacy). One may think "I live by the sword, die by the sword," but no lives can determine that. And there's the thrill of victory on one side of the coin and an agony of defeat. I won't pretend that it doesn't feel good to know I'm on a winning streak. But the game is still in the making. I won't subject my focus to my winning record, because it may cause me to fall short. I'm reminded of the season when my grandson J-Bird and his football team the Broncos...

Went undefeated right up to the championship. Only

the B-Team lost to the Cowboys, who won the year before. My grandson was on the B-Team, and he was frustrated to the point of crying. I told him in so many words and in my own words, “Live to fight another day.” I let J-Bird know that there’s a risk in having a perfect record because one doesn’t know what it is to lose. Then, when we experience a loss, we can better prepare. I’m reminded of one of my favorite NFL teams, The Steelers. They went 11-0 last year (2020) then lost their first. I hoped for it to be a running season for the Super Bowl. I’m reminded that my level of success has been determined by my past failures. But this has also trained me in knowing what to look for or expect next around the pitfalls of temptation. There’s no individual that hasn’t had something to show for except money and drugs. As it states, “to win souls is wise.” Let us be fishers of men.

In a world where every move is a calculated step, I’m reminded to keep my hand on the trigger. As soon as my eyes are open to witness another day, this war has already been won, but dark forces still battle to lose. They’re a defeated foe that can put on a pretty good bluff, like in poker games—smoke screens that challenge the content of our character. But as long as we know who we belong to and how rare, we will keep the cutting edge. This will continue to give us favor with the Lord.

We as a people need to feel and be safe as the watchmen of the tower. Being our keepers, we have the ability to fulfill the calling in the sight of the Lord. When all this becomes a bunch of rules (Do's and Don'ts), we will suffer a burnout. We are compelled to delight ourselves in the things of God, meaning having no desire to be the generation of movers and shakers passed down. I'm learning to fall in love with directing the lesser to the right path, and as long as I live, I find more room to grow in the things of God. And in doing so, we are continually saving ourselves. This should be our ultimate aim to clear all confusion. It starts by exercising an attitude of integrity. Remember, our Father is the all-seeing eye, and He desires to bring us to a state of openness to get His finished work done. Christ won't return until everyone has the opportunity to yield or reject. The question is, are we truly leading or being led into question and landing it? There should be power in our actions. Let us stay up and be the priest of this last-day movement.

We should know that the world was designed to give us the essentials to bring out the best of who God is. This means even after the Fall of Man in the garden, God provided a way through Jesus in which we can get the finished work done. I watch my fingers and toes how many times I've witnessed evil that opposes unseen to make their presence known when the Word of God is going forth. The spirit of distraction fights against the spirit of doubt to cause confusion, to keep positive energy to fall on the hearers to birth a new miracle. Souls are released when the power of the Lord makes its presence known. We are agents or host to represent who we are in Christ by walking in the Spirit, which matches up with our spirit man to do God's will. This is the whole duty of man. Everything else is secondary. Let us exercise our free-will to influence a dying world that's looking for an answer. I'm reminded that "Man's extremities are God's opportunity," and God uses ordinary people to do extraordinary things. One can make a difference. May we learn our identity in Christ before we let the problem be the solution instead of finding the madness. Let us major in minors to be equipped to tackle the more advanced problems. Let us view problems as math equations that can be solved. Problems that can be solved by being broken down.

To its lowest terms — God majors on keeping things simple for us. The sheep of His pasture. May we keep a sheep mentality, which means we are motivated only by the voice of the shepherd. Where, like real sheep, we follow where we are led, making for peace, not drinking from notorious waters such as people, places, and things. We are equipped to distinguish between the voice of deception vs. a sound plan of action. Not building a house of confusion, including followers. Followers rather seek a sermon vs. learning one. We are trained to recognize truth vs. error. This is important (the first rule of thumb). Otherwise, you know, truth can be added that can fool the best of us. Let us remain humble to continue to be true students of the Bible, which will give us the cutting edge to determine students who aren't real. A good teacher or shepherd can resume the role of a student or follower if the person who accepted it can pierce the darkness and expose that which is fake. This will increase the following opportunities, which will create a massive transformation. People have lost or misplaced their zeal or enthusiasm. It's important to wake up our minds, which will separate the wheat from the weeds. Then we can clear the air. Be encouraged.

There is never a dull moment in the things of God. Things to let go and things to embrace (out with the old and in with the new). But be reminded that many of the things considered new may have been born in a different skin or time. History does repeat itself. It's just a different inhabitants passed on from generations, but let us promote generational blessings that will last a lifetime. Our world is small in the eyes of the beholder. Let us carry a big stick to remind us that we may tremble the many. Remember our forefathers who saw Canaan as a land that could and was for the taking. The question is, do we want to eat and live or starve and go home hungry? No bell of pity to die setting an example of failure. Remember, we are the great example of witnesses. So, choose whom you will serve, God or the things of God. It's time to look back and be reminded that everything that shuck is of value. And our honor or conduct of character is priceless. Let us continue to be the last-day generations of those who walk by faith. Those to behold chariots of fire, not as mere tourists but leave a mark of thunder upon the blacktop. The Elijah and Elisha effect. Be there!

As we supply the world with a solution that's simple, it's plain to use that we as humans need to be the ones who aren't the creators or founders of things we had no reverence for from the beginning. It's just the act of disobedience that clouds the judgment. The recipe for dwelling and relationship with the Creator is love and obedience. "Love" and "obedience" are the confidence that will follow. David, in his shepherd state of being, was confident to not be defeated because of past victories with a bear or lion. Each triumph experience will develop a purpose-driven vs. flee or give up. One acts of defeat in their lives, and we will encourage witnesses to have hope. "Hope" is an attribute that breeds “Faith.” In a rule of a nation or deliverers that were set to cover the finish work, it takes preparation for every victory and record of success. Every generation has a story to tell. A cloudy start or finish will not be subject to hang. Though we see through a dimmer, yet will clear like a steady stream that shows the wounds of battle. It will heal like victory without laboring body and mind. To see that the broken-hearted upon being built a story of comeback and a comeback shows determination. The world is decaying, but there is medicine. Ask your neighbor; spiritual guides will be remembered, everyone is evaluated.

As the world turns, it brings about lessons that are learned or should be. Nevertheless, we can observe the making of many tales. This is to the training of the eye that we expect what they put into something. We've learned to decrease so that our spirit quality increases. We're learning to conduct ourselves out of the darkness. Memories tasked us to the Most High. I speak in terms of our encounters with forces that will or will not pierce who are oppressed as those who don't oppose themselves on how to engage with as well as possessed. Jesus said that they don't know themselves, their identity, or their thoughts, creating a motion of influence that isn't their own spirit, but of darkness. He was able to identify the failure. Life's lessons will expose those who are righteous and who aren't. Pressure comes after we face what we know. A whole life lesson will teach us the nature of others. This is the following, to love God is sound, and we learn dangerous knowledge and fellowship, to love God is sound, and we learn more to be. Let us not infarct who we don't see, nor discard who we make will of. This is how not to haste our fellowships. Make will of it, and this is how not to hold onto our mistakes. This is how not to haste our fellowship and error our wings. The movement of love was designed; it was. We reassure ourselves to exercise this moment. Love breeds our atmosphere of peace, we will throw out there, and the same we will return. Like the atmosphere of peace, in return. A circle of peace will move through thoughts, becoming easier for us to sleep.

Every day we blossom in our faith as we allow the attributes that allow us to grow and the flaws that teach us as people. Holiness to people lets an opportunity arise in its simplest forms. Let's not free course what people do or else we dismiss destruction. And this can be considered when we ignore the warning signs. God always sends His merciful signals before destruction.

As I continue not to grow cold, we must guard our hearts before destruction may come. The more I witness, the more we keep our hearts on important spiritual things and feed off the warnings that tell us to join in. I see that it's important to join the race. We are not too distant from the prize. Being sensitive to the spirit has come to those who are led and have shown sensitivity to God. I speak of this from my heart as we prepare ourselves to break our downward slope and not give up spiritually. If I had to compare beyond this, I would say we need to beware. I think of the prayers (people) who repair their lives and ruin it. Be aware of those who only think of themselves, who fail to fix themselves.

As we continue to learn to walk on water, we become lifeguards of souls as we secure our own. Walking on water is a progressive act, and it's a life-long experience that is challenged every day by the forces of darkness that are instigated by those who are adversaries, who improperly pass their failures, which are inherited from birth but need to be developed by awareness. The Holy Spirit teaches us how to walk on water, which is essential for survival in a world that promotes blindness because they want to keep prisoners. But we learn who we are to expel darkness, to enable us to exercise our ability to usher in the second advent. We are blood-bought, which means there is a responsibility to pierce the darkness. Let's not be idle; the time between our salvation depends on it. As we look through the eyes of God, we will see that everything He has made is good, but labeled during the fall of man. But, like He set restoration through Jesus, then through us, the order extends His rightful hand of fellowship to all mankind. May we all have five loaves, two fishes, and the same thanks as He met our needs as we partake. We are the children of His on earth. He has the whole world to treat.

Let us not become weary, as this replicates us as fastened into a stance that the Lord is God!

As we walk on water and secure our salvation, we empower our abilities to expand our territory with people, places, and things. There is strength in our hearts when we heed the voice of gratitude, which is pressing the works of God. We are compelled to ensure we are on the rise for our godly efforts toward man. To recognize that there's a spiritual world of beings, first and foremost, allows us to pay circumstances to the obedience favorable to a positive scene. This makes a life to be in harmony with God and the angels that protect us. Our guardian angels work firsthand to help and give us access to the throne room of God. We can move and have our way by allowing God through the Holy Spirit to have free course in us. This simply means to be sensitive to the things of God. The atmosphere of God is created by choosing the things of God, such as Biblical readings, the holy Bible, and being in the presence of people who exercise their faith in Christ. Let us continue to be on the winning team that is leading ways to continue raising a higher bar by standing by or showing a higher level of dedication to live under the radar of a place that is overrated. Too much emphasis has been invested in this world that has little deposited but expects more in return.

Prayer :

Lord, I thank You for last night's kind protection and provision. I ask for forgiveness for my transgressions. I pray I can walk in Your blessings today. I ask that my family and I could be a blessing to others. Keep my heart and mind focused on You throughout the day. Shield my thoughts and actions from the world. Lord, help me fulfill Your purpose for my life today. I am trusting myself to You. I choose to pursue Your goodness today. Amen.

As we begin to organize and exercise the positions in life, God has given us; we can better reflect the nature of God. This gives us the awareness of how important "time" plays in our lives. I become more power-driven to erase all appearances of evil. We must keep in mind that as representatives of God, the forces of darkness will cater to us with luxuries that once may have seemed not enticing. This can be because that which was going unnoticed but now visible is apparent. Darkness can no longer hide or disguise itself. We can then land in a manner that pleases God and provides comfort to us and those who were influenced. We are the winning team that can better exercise our skills by showing our offensive behavior vs. our defensive. This I mean, let us take it to the enemy forces with a plan of action to dissolve their walls. Just as when the walls of Jericho were led to ruin, so be it for any lines of defense that come against us. There are walls as lines of defense to keep out evil, so are there walls that serve as keeping the common man and harvest from receiving deliverance from strongholds. But the breaking of the Holy Word we exercise can and will break all bondages. And the more we use and exercise them, the greater we can pierce the darkness. Light expels darkness to continue our quest to secure our freedom. This is my contribution to when all else fails we can learn to walk on water meaning to release a faith that gets the job done. Because without faith it's impossible to please God.

Pastor ; Derrick Lacy SDA.

www.ingramcontent.com/pod-product-compliance
Lightning Source LLC
LaVergne TN
LVHW091241150826
845673LV00003B/1244

* 9 7 9 8 8 9 5 6 9 4 2 5 1 *